Our Lady of Sorrows

DEVOTION TO
MARY'S SEVEN SORROWS
FOR CHILDREN

Our Lady
of
SORROWS

WRITTEN BY PATRICK O'HEARN
ILLUSTRATED BY ADALEE HUDE

Foreword by
Fr. Chad Ripperger, Ph.D.

SOPHIA INSTITUTE PRESS
Manchester, New Hampshire

Sophia Institute Press

Box 5284, Manchester, NH 03108

1-800-888-9344

www.SophiaInstitute.com

Sophia Institute Press is a registered trademark of Sophia Institute.

hardcover ISBN 979-8-88911-200-6

ebook ISBN 979-8-88911-201-3

Library of Congress Control Number: 2023952034

First printing

This book is lovingly dedicated to my godchildren:
Bridget O'Hearn, Robert Vidmar,
Margaret O'Hearn, and Bella Johanni.
— P. O.

This book is lovingly dedicated to my godson,
Logan Anthony Wurts.
— A. H.

Contents

Foreword

In the living room of my parents' home is a picture of Michelangelo's *Pietà*. From the earliest age, I would study the picture from time to time. What always struck me was Our Lady's incomparable beauty, even in the midst of the agony of embracing her Son's dead body. I admired equally her unwavering fidelity to her Son, regardless of the suffering that would entail. Whether it is due to Michelangelo's artistic ability to capture living events or to Our Sorrowful Mother's perpetual and unfailing inseparability from her Son, the picture seems almost timeless, despite hanging on the wall for five decades.

Even young children have the capacity for compassion, and we see this when they view the suffering of a friend or a family member. The devotion to Our Lady of Sorrows can be fostered in children even at the tenderest of ages. Parents can incite in their children a true love for Our Lady by helping them to appreciate the suffering she endured in order to remain faithful to her Son and to the will of God the Father. And after reaching the age of reason, according to their age and capacity, children can be taught about the struggle that we all endure in the spiritual battle and Our Lady's promise of protection to those who practice a devotion to her under the title of Sorrowful Mother. Additionally, under the title of Sorrowful Mother, she will often reveal to those who have this devotion things that they need to know. So by fostering in your children a devotion to Our Lady, you will help them learn to turn to her for answers regarding their vocation and regarding what they need to address to advance in the spiritual life; and through the Holy Spirit's gift of knowledge, they will see with conviction the truths of the Catholic Faith.

Saying the seven Hail Marys daily will help to cultivate a long-lasting devotion to Our Lady as well as a deepening attachment to the Passion and death of Our Lord, to which Our Lady is inextricably linked. The prayers contained in this book provide good examples for children in how to pray to Our Lady for those spiritual needs. As with each prior generation, parents would be well served to foster in their children a strong devotion to Our Lady.

—Fr. Chad Ripperger, Ph.D.

Introduction

There are many devotions in the Catholic Church, but there is none so simple and yet so powerful as praying seven Hail Marys to console the heart of Our Lady of Sorrows. You might have seen images of the Immaculate Heart of Mary pierced by seven swords. Each of those swords represents one of Our Lady's Seven Sorrows.

The Seven Sorrows are as follows:

1. The prophecy of Simeon (Luke 2:34–35)
2. The flight into Egypt (Matthew 2:13–14)
3. The loss of the Child Jesus in the Temple (Luke 2:41–45)
4. Mary meets Jesus on the way to Calvary (Luke 23:27–28)
5. Jesus dies on the Cross (John 19:25–27)
6. Mary receives the dead body of Jesus in her arms (John 19:38–40)
7. Jesus is placed in the tomb (John 19:41–42)

Our Lady told St. Bridget of Sweden that she would grant the following graces to those who pray and meditate on her Seven Sorrows daily:

1. I will grant peace to their families.
2. They will be enlightened about the divine mysteries.
3. I will console them in their pains, and I will accompany them in their work.

4. I will give them as much as they ask for, as long as it does not oppose the adorable will of my divine Son or the sanctification of their souls.

5. I will defend them in their spiritual battles with the infernal enemy, and I will protect them at every instant of their lives.

6. I will visibly help them at the moment of their death; they will see the face of their Mother.

7. I have obtained from my divine Son that those who propagate this devotion to my tears and dolors will be taken directly from this earthly life to eternal happiness, since all their sins will be forgiven, and my Son and I will be their eternal consolation and joy.

To console Mary's heart is to console Jesus' heart, for both hearts beat for each other. In this book, you will find the Scripture references to the Seven Sorrows accompanied by beautiful images, reflections, and prayers. May all who read this book, both young and old, be inspired to love Our Lady's sorrowful heart with the greatest devotion. Those who practice this powerful devotion will have Mary's protection "at every instant of their lives," but especially "at the moment of their death."

Our Lady of Sorrows, pray for us!

Our Lady of Sorrows

The prophecy of Simeon

....

And Simeon blessed them and said to Mary
his mother, "Behold, this child is set for the
fall and rising of many in Israel, and for a sign
that is spoken against (and a sword will pierce
through your own soul also), that thoughts
out of many hearts may be revealed."

—Luke 2:34–35

OUR LADY

My child, when Simeon said these words, the first sword pierced my heart. I knew I could not protect my Son from His future trials. Instead, I had to prepare Him to be courageous. As I looked down at His tiny fingers and His chubby cheeks, my Immaculate Heart ached with so much love for Him.

Like God the Father, I also could say, "I so loved the world that I gave my only Son." Please offer a Hail Mary to console my sorrowful heart.

HAIL MARY
English & Latin

Hail Mary, full of grace, the Lord is with thee; blessed are thou among women, and blessed is the fruit of thy womb, Jesus. Holy Mary, Mother of God, pray for us sinners, now and at the hour of our death. Amen.

Ave, María, grátia plena, Dóminus tecum. Benedícta tu in muliéribus, et benedíctus fructus ventris tui, Iesus. Sancta María, Mater Dei, ora pro nobis peccatóribus, nunc et in hora mortis nostrae. Amen.

PRAYER

O Blessed Mother, Our Lady of Sorrows, you who knew the prophecies from the moment your Son was born—that your Son would offer His life for souls—help me to bear my crosses. Help me to have courage to face the future with faith, hope, and courage, not doubt, negativity, and discouragement. I ask this in the name of your Son, Jesus Christ, Our Lord. Amen.

The flight into Egypt

....

Now when they had departed, behold, an angel of the Lord appeared to Joseph in a dream and said, "Rise, take the child and his mother, and flee to Egypt, and remain there till I tell you; for Herod is about to search for the child, to destroy him." And he rose and took the child and his mother by night, and departed to Egypt.

—Matthew 2:13–14

OUR LADY

My child, when my husband, St. Joseph, told me to flee with him and Jesus to Egypt, I obeyed immediately. Can you imagine leaving your homeland in the middle of the night because a very evil king was trying to harm your family? Can you imagine walking more than eighty miles to another country through a cold, windy desert? Can you imagine being separated from your relatives for many years? God asked this sacrifice of my family, and we made it because we loved God and trusted Him completely. Please offer a Hail Mary to console my sorrowful heart.

HAIL MARY
English & Latin

Hail Mary, full of grace, the Lord is with thee; blessed are thou among women, and blessed is the fruit of thy womb, Jesus. Holy Mary, Mother of God, pray for us sinners, now and at the hour of our death. Amen.

Ave, María, grátia plena, Dóminus tecum. Benedicta tu in muliéribus, et benedíctus fructus ventris tui, Iesus. Sancta María, Mater Dei, ora pro nobis peccatóribus, nunc et in hora mortis nostrae. Amen.

PRAYER

O Blessed Mother, Our Lady of Sorrows, you who left everything behind to take your Son to Egypt, help me to go wherever God leads me. Help me to be obedient to my parents, as you were obedient to St. Joseph. Walk with me on my long journey as I walk through this valley of tears. Lead me to the mountain of Heaven as I learn to let go of earthly things. I ask this in the name of your Son, Jesus Christ, Our Lord. Amen.

The loss of the Child Jesus in the Temple

Now his parents went to Jerusalem every year at the feast of the Passover. And when he was twelve years old, they went up according to custom; and when the feast was ended, as they were returning, the boy Jesus stayed behind in Jerusalem. His parents did not know it, but supposing him to be in the company they went a day's journey, and they sought him among their kinsfolk and acquaintances; and when they did not find him, they returned to Jerusalem, seeking him.

—Luke 2:41-45

OUR LADY

My child, when St. Joseph and I lost Jesus for three days, our hearts were filled with great sadness, for we did not know if we would ever see Him again. You might have felt a similar pain if you were ever lost and could not find your parents. You might have become frightened and worried that you would never see them again. And your parents would have felt the same way about you. How our hearts were filled with joy when we found Jesus! Please offer a Hail Mary to console my sorrowful heart.

HAIL MARY

English & Latin

Hail Mary, full of grace, the Lord is with thee; blessed are thou among women, and blessed is the fruit of thy womb, Jesus. Holy Mary, Mother of God, pray for us sinners, now and at the hour of our death. Amen.

Ave, María, grátia plena, Dóminus tecum. Benedicta tu in muliéribus, et benedíctus fructus ventris tui, Iesus. Sancta María, Mater Dei, ora pro nobis peccatóribus, nunc et in hora mortis nostrae. Amen.

PRAYER

O Blessed Mother, Our Lady of Sorrows, you who lost Jesus for three days in the Temple, help me to keep my soul always in a state of grace so that I may never lose Jesus. Whenever I wander from your Son through sin, please lead me back to Him. I ask this in the name of your Son, Jesus Christ, Our Lord. Amen.

Mary meets Jesus on the way to Calvary

And there followed him a great multitude of
the people, and of women who bewailed and
lamented him. But Jesus turning to them said,
"Daughters of Jerusalem, do not weep for me;
but weep for yourselves and for your children."

—Luke 23:27–28

Our Lady

My child, as Jesus carried His heavy Cross, I wanted nothing more than to carry it for Him. I wanted to help Him, but I felt so helpless. Every time He fell to the ground, my heart broke anew. I recalled when He fell as a child while learning to walk. I know that Jesus' pain only increased when He saw my pain. I had to follow Him to Calvary, and you, too, must follow Him to reach Heaven. Please offer a Hail Mary to console my sorrowful heart.

Hail Mary

English & Latin

Hail Mary, full of grace, the Lord is with thee; blessed are thou among women, and blessed is the fruit of thy womb, Jesus. Holy Mary, Mother of God, pray for us sinners, now and at the hour of our death. Amen.

Ave, María, grátia plena, Dóminus tecum. Benedícta tu in muliéribus, et benedíctus fructus ventris tui, Iesus. Sancta María, Mater Dei, ora pro nobis peccatóribus, nunc et in hora mortis nostrae. Amen.

Prayer

O Blessed Mother, Our Lady of Sorrows, you who followed Jesus on the Way of the Cross, suffering with Him in body and soul, help me to follow Him to Calvary. Let me focus on His pain and not my pain. I ask this in the name of your Son, Jesus Christ, Our Lord. Amen.

Jesus dies on the Cross

Standing by the cross of Jesus were his mother, and his mother's sister, Mary the wife of Clopas, and Mary Magdalene. When Jesus saw his mother, and the disciple whom he loved standing near, he said to his mother, "Woman, behold, your son!" Then he said to the disciple, "Behold, your mother!" And from that hour the disciple took her to his own home.

—John 19:25–27

OUR LADY

My child, as I saw Jesus on the Cross, my eyes were filled with an ocean of tears. I could not even recognize Him; He had wounds all over His body. St. John the Evangelist was the only apostle who didn't leave Him. I needed to be strong for my Son, so I stood by Him at the foot of the Cross. Won't you stay with my Son too? For the only joy is to be near Jesus. Please offer a Hail Mary to console my sorrowful heart.

HAIL MARY

English & Latin

Hail Mary, full of grace, the Lord is with thee; blessed are thou among women, and blessed is the fruit of thy womb, Jesus. Holy Mary, Mother of God, pray for us sinners, now and at the hour of our death. Amen.

Ave, María, grátia plena, Dóminus tecum. Benedícta tu in muliéribus, et benedíctus fructus ventris tui, Iesus. Sancta María, Mater Dei, ora pro nobis peccatóribus, nunc et in hora mortis nostrae. Amen.

PRAYER

O Blessed Mother, Our Lady of Sorrows, you who stood at the foot of the Cross, help me always to stand by Jesus and never leave Him. Remain with me when I am suffering and bring me your Son's peace during my trials. I ask this in the name of your Son, Jesus Christ, Our Lord. Amen.

Mary receives the dead body of Jesus in her arms

....

After this, Joseph of Arimathea, who was a disciple of Jesus, but secretly, for fear of the Jews, asked Pilate that he might take away the body of Jesus, and Pilate gave him leave. So he came and took away his body. Nicodemus also, who had at first come to him by night, came bringing a mixture of myrrh and aloes, about a hundred pounds' weight. They took the body of Jesus, and bound it in linen cloths with the spices, as is the burial custom of the Jews.

—John 19:38–40

OUR LADY

My child, as Jesus was placed in my arms for the last time, I held Him with the most tender love as I kissed His sacred wounds. And as I cradled Him in my arms, I thought about the first time I held Him in Bethlehem. How I longed for those blessed days to hold Him once more as a child. But God had willed that my Son, our God, must die for the sins of all people. Please offer a Hail Mary to console my sorrowful heart.

HAIL MARY

English & Latin

Hail Mary, full of grace, the Lord is with thee; blessed are thou among women, and blessed is the fruit of thy womb, Jesus. Holy Mary, Mother of God, pray for us sinners, now and at the hour of our death. Amen.

Ave, María, grátia plena, Dóminus tecum. Benedícta tu in muliéribus, et benedíctus fructus ventris tui, Iesus. Sancta María, Mater Dei, ora pro nobis peccatóribus, nunc et in hora mortis nostrae. Amen.

PRAYER

O Blessed Mother, Our Lady of Sorrows, you who so lovingly held the Savior of the world in Bethlehem and on Calvary, please kiss Jesus' sacred wounds for me. Hold me always in your mantle, and let me never be separated from your Son. I ask this in the name of your Son, Jesus Christ, Our Lord. Amen.

Jesus is placed in the tomb

Now in the place where he was crucified there was a garden, and in the garden a new tomb where no one had ever been laid. So because of the Jewish day of Preparation, as the tomb was close at hand, they laid Jesus there.

—John 19:41–42

OUR LADY

My child, just as I once swaddled my Son as a baby, so now I had to cover Him one last time with a burial shroud. I did not want to let go of my Son; I wanted to hold Him forever in my arms. I never wanted to leave Him. But I had to let Him go so that He could rise from the dead so that you and I could be with Him one day in Heaven. How happy we will all be in Heaven with Jesus! Please offer a Hail Mary to console my sorrowful heart.

HAIL MARY

English & Latin

Hail Mary, full of grace, the Lord is with thee; blessed are thou among women, and blessed is the fruit of thy womb, Jesus. Holy Mary, Mother of God, pray for us sinners, now and at the hour of our death. Amen.

Ave, María, grátia plena, Dóminus tecum. Benedícta tu in muliéribus, et benedíctus fructus ventris tui, Iesus. Sancta María, Mater Dei, ora pro nobis peccatóribus, nunc et in hora mortis nostrae. Amen.

PRAYER

O Blessed Mother, Our Lady of Sorrows, your tears fell to the ground like raindrops at the sight of your Son being placed in the tomb. When the stone was sealed, the final sword pierced your heart, because you did not want to leave Him. Help me to love Jesus above everything so that I might be with Him and you in Heaven. Help me always to have hope in the Resurrection. I ask this in the name of your Son, Jesus Christ, Our Lord. Amen.

Litany of Our Lady of the Seven Sorrows

By Servant of God Pope Pius VII

Lord, have mercy on us.

Christ, have mercy on us.

Lord, have mercy on us. Christ, hear us.

Christ, graciously hear us.

God the Father of Heaven, *have mercy on us.*

God the Son, Redeemer of the world, *have mercy on us.*

God the Holy Spirit, *have mercy on us.*

Holy Trinity, one God, *have mercy on us.*

Holy Mary, *pray for us.*

Holy Mother of God, *pray for us.*

Holy Virgin of virgins, *pray for us.*

Mother of the Crucified, *pray for us.*

Sorrowful Mother, *pray for us.*

Mournful Mother, *pray for us.*

Sighing Mother, *pray for us.*

Afflicted Mother, *pray for us.*

Desolate Mother, *pray for us.*

Mother most sad, *pray for us.*

Mother set around with anguish, *pray for us.*

Mother overwhelmed by grief, *pray for us.*

Mother transfixed by a sword, *pray for us.*

Mother crucified in thy heart, *pray for us.*

Mother bereaved of thy Son, *pray for us.*

Sighing Dove, *pray for us.*

Mother of Dolors, *pray for us.*

Fount of tears, *pray for us.*

Sea of bitterness, *pray for us.*

Field of tribulation, *pray for us.*

Mass of suffering, *pray for us.*

Mirror of patience, *pray for us.*

Rock of constancy, *pray for us.*

Remedy in perplexity, *pray for us.*

Joy of the afflicted, *pray for us.*

Ark of the desolate, *pray for us.*

Refuge of the abandoned, *pray for us.*

Shield of the oppressed, *pray for us.*

Conqueror of the incredulous, *pray for us.*

Solace of the wretched, *pray for us.*

Medicine of the sick, *pray for us.*

Help of the faint, *pray for us.*

Strength of the weak, *pray for us.*

Protectress of those who fight, *pray for us.*

Haven of the shipwrecked, *pray for us.*

Calmer of tempests, *pray for us.*

Companion of the sorrowful, *pray for us.*

Retreat of those who groan, *pray for us.*

Terror of the treacherous, *pray for us.*

Standard-bearer of the martyrs, *pray for us.*

Treasure of the faithful, *pray for us.*

Light of confessors, *pray for us.*

Pearl of virgins, *pray for us.*

Comfort of widows, *pray for us.*

Joy of all saints, *pray for us.*

Queen of thy servants, *pray for us.*

Holy Mary, who alone art unexampled, *pray for us.*

Pray for us, most Sorrowful Virgin,
that we may be made worthy of the promises of Christ.

Let us pray.
O God, in whose Passion,
according to the prophecy of Simeon,
a sword of grief pierced through the most sweet soul
of Thy glorious Blessed Virgin Mother, Mary:
grant that we, who celebrate the memory of her Seven Sorrows,
may obtain the happy effect of Thy Passion,
who lives and reigns world without end. Amen.

Traditional Prayers for Children

···································

SIGN OF THE CROSS

In the Name of the Father, and of the Son and of the Holy Spirit. Amen.

In Nómine Patris, et Fílii, et Spíritus Sancti. Amen.

OUR FATHER

Our Father, who art in Heaven, hallowed be Thy name; Thy kingdom come; Thy will be done, on earth as it is in Heaven. Give us this day our daily bread, and forgive us our trespasses as we forgive those who trespass against us. And lead us not into temptation, but deliver us from evil. Amen.

Pater noster, qui es in caelis, sanctificétur nomen tuum; advéniat regnum tuum; fiat volúntas tua, sicut in caelo et in terra. Panem nostrum quotidiánum da nobis hódie, et dimítte nobis débita nostra, sicut et nos dimíttimus debitóribus nostris. Et ne nos indúcas in tentatiónem sed líbera nos a malo. Amen.

Hail Mary

Hail Mary, full of grace, the Lord is with thee; blessed are thou among women, and blessed is the fruit of thy womb, Jesus. Holy Mary, Mother of God, pray for us sinners, now and at the hour of our death. Amen.

Ave, María, grátia plena, Dóminus tecum. Benedícta tu in muliéribus, et benedíctus fructus ventris tui, Iesus. Sancta María, Mater Dei, ora pro nobis peccatóribus, nunc et in hora mortis nostrae. Amen.

Glory Be

Glory be to the Father, and to the Son, and to the Holy Spirit; as it was in the beginning, is now, and ever shall be, world without end. Amen.

Glória Patri, et Fílio, et Spíritui Sancto; sicut erat in princípio, et nunc, et semper, et in saecula saeculórum. Amen.

Angel of God

Angel of God, my guardian dear, to whom God's love commits me here, ever this day be at my side, to light and guard, to rule and guide. Amen.

Ángele Dei, qui custos es mei, me tibi commissum pietáte supérna, hodie illúmina, custódi, rege, et gubérna. Amen.

Prayer to St. Michael the Archangel

St. Michael the Archangel, defend us in battle; be our protection against the wickedness and snares of the devil. May God rebuke him, we humbly pray; and do thou, O prince of the heavenly host, by the power of God, thrust into Hell Satan and all the evil spirits who prowl about the world seeking the ruin of souls. Amen.

Sáncte Míchael Archángele, defénde nos in proélio, cóntra nequítiam et insídias diáboli ésto praesídium. Ímperet ílli Déus, súpplices deprecámur: tuque, prínceps milítiae caeléstis, Sátanam aliósque spíritus malígnos, qui ad perditiónem animárum pervagántur in múndo, divína virtúte, in inférnum detrúde. Amen.

Other Daily Prayers

By Fr. Chad Ripperger, Ph.D.

....

Daily Prayer for My Vocation

Dear Jesus, give me Thy light and grace to find the vocation that Thou wills for me. Grant me courage to follow Thy will, so that I might become a saint and live with Thee in Heaven. Surround me with Thy heavenly angels and saints and with the mantle of Our Blessed Mother. Amen.

Daily Prayer for Protection

Dear Jesus, I ask Thee to protect me and my family from all harm, accidents, and sickness. Send Thy holy angels to guard me and my family. St. Michael and my guardian angel, defend me from all the wickedness and snares of the devil. Amen.

Daily Prayer to Mary

Dear Blessed Mother, Our Lady of Sorrows, I choose thee this day as my protectress. Keep me from every sin and especially from the evil spirits. Help me to love thy Son as thou loves Him. I place in thy hands everything that I am and everything that I love, for thy Son's glory. Amen.

Nightly Prayer of Gratitude

Dear Jesus, I thank Thee for all the blessings and graces Thou has given me this day, especially for the Holy Eucharist, Our Lady, my guardian angel, and my family. I ask Thee to drive away all the demons that might affect me while I sleep. I offer my sleep for Thy glory. Amen.

About the Author and Illustrator

Patrick O'Hearn is a husband and a father. He holds a master's degree in education from Franciscan University. He has authored or co-authored seven books, including *Parents of the Saints*, *Nursery of Heaven* (co-author), *The Shepherd at the Crib and the Cross*, *Courtship of the Saints*, *The Grief of Dads* (co-author), and *Go and Fear Nothing*. You can visit his website at patrickrohearn.com.

Wife, mom, artist, and Catholic author Adalee Hude calls her little artistic corner Brightly Hude Studio. Fueled largely by prayer and tea, she has done illustration work for Catholic magazines, prayer journals, stickers, and several Catholic children's books, all for the greater glory of God. Find her work at BrightlyHude.com.

About

SOPHIA INSTITUTE

Sophia Institute is a nonprofit institution that seeks to nurture the spiritual, moral, and cultural life of souls and to spread the Gospel of Christ in conformity with the authentic teachings of the Roman Catholic Church.

Sophia Institute Press fulfills this mission by offering translations, reprints, and new publications that afford readers a rich source of the enduring wisdom of mankind.

Sophia Institute also operates the popular online resource Catholic-Exchange.com. Catholic Exchange provides world news from a Catholic perspective as well as daily devotionals and articles that will help readers to grow in holiness and live a life consistent with the teachings of the Church.

In 2013, Sophia Institute launched Sophia Institute for Teachers to renew and rebuild Catholic culture through service to Catholic education. With the goal of nurturing the spiritual, moral, and cultural life of souls, and an abiding respect for the role and work of teachers, we strive to provide materials and programs that are at once enlightening to the mind and ennobling to the heart; faithful and complete, as well as useful and practical.

Sophia Institute gratefully recognizes the Solidarity Association for preserving and encouraging the growth of our apostolate over the course of many years. Without their generous and timely support, this book would not be in your hands.

www.SophiaInstitute.com
www.CatholicExchange.com
www.SophiaInstituteforTeachers.org